# The Victim

MIKE WILSON

# CHAPTER ONE

Two of us.
Dazz and me.

It was evening, just gone dark.

We walked without a sound,
down the middle of the road.

We passed the corner shop,
quiet and empty.
We passed the taxi on bricks.

We wore black.

Dazz was the leader.
He carried the big screwdriver
hidden in his jacket.

"Don't forget, Slim," he said.
"Two minutes max.
Then we get out."

I nodded.

One house was quiet and dark.
You could tell no-one was at home.

"That one," said Dazz.
He slipped down the side of the house,
into the shadows.

I waited a second,
looking up and down the street.
Nothing.

Then I went after Dazz
into the darkness.

I found him
working the big screwdriver
under the frame of the back window.

There was a lock on it,
but not for long.

Dazz swung down hard,
pulling on the screwdriver
with his powerful arms.
The window sprang open
with a loud SNAP!
and the crack of splitting wood.

I put my foot in his hands
and Dazz lifted me up.

I held the window open,
and slipped head first
into the cool, dark room.

There was a table under the window.
I landed on it
as I fell into the room.

I was in. So far, so good.

I went quickly to the back door
to let Dazz in.

"Now go! Run! RUN!"
He pushed me into the next room.

If the house was empty,
noise didn't matter that much.
Speed mattered.
Getting in, getting out.

I ran upstairs.
Dazz went to the front door,
and slid the bolt to lock it.
Then he went to work
in the living room.

I ran into a bedroom
and threw open the drawers and cupboards.
Clothes, a woman's clothes, and make-up.
Nothing of value.

In a box by the side of the bed,
I found some rings and other jewellery.

Not bad, but not that good.
I put them all in my pocket.

In the other bedroom there was a desk,
and lots of books,
books and papers everywhere.

I found a camera,
and a Walkman and headphones.
I put them under my jacket.

There was some money in a dish:
notes and coins. I took that too.

I could hear Dazz downstairs,
calling me quietly:
"Slim! Two minutes!
Time to go!"

And then I saw her.

On the desk was a letter
and a photograph.
The letter said:

> To Jan,
>
> here is that photo I took of you,
> looking gorgeous as usual!
> Hope it cheers you up!
> love David   X

The woman in the photograph was smiling,
and holding a glass of wine,
and looking right at me.

So much love.

Suddenly,
everything was confused.
What I was doing
in this woman's house?

Why was I trying to steal from her?

She was so beautiful,
the way she was looking at me
from the photograph.
She was so beautiful,
I couldn't take my eyes off her.

Dazz was calling me again.

"Slim!
Bring what you've got and let's go!"

I put down the camera,
and the Walkman
and the money and the jewellery.

I wanted to keep the photograph.
But I couldn't think straight.
I think I must have dropped it,
or left it there.

"Slim for God's sake!
Come on!
Let's get out NOW!"

"OK. OK.!" I shouted back at him.

I ran downstairs
and Dazz and I left the house.

He was mad with me
as we walked away.

"What kept you?
What did you get?"

I didn't look at him.

"Nothing.
I looked everywhere.
There was nothing to steal."

Dazz kept looking at me,
but I didn't care if he believed me or not.

All I cared about was Jan
and the photograph I had left behind.

I knew I had to see her again.

# CHAPTER TWO

"I was on a late shift,"
Jan told the police woman
"Two till ten."

It wasn't cold in the house,
but she sat holding herself.

"If I know I will be late,
I always leave a light on,
but this time I forgot.

"When I got home,
they had locked my front door.
I couldn't get in my own house."

The police woman nodded and smiled.
Her radio crackled and spat,
but she took no notice.
They sat in silence.

Two cups of tea
were going cold on the table.

The policeman came down from upstairs.

"Odd. Very odd." he said.

"No fingerprints, very professional.
They knew what they were doing.
But in the back bedroom,
your camera, your rings and things,
all left on the desk.

"They found the jewellery,
carried it through from one room to the other,
and left it in a pile in there...

"I wonder why?"

When the police had gone,
Jan went upstairs
and put all her things away again:
her clothes, her letters.

On the floor by the desk,
she saw the photograph
her brother David had taken
in Italy last year.

Hope it cheers you up!

She tore it into pieces and put them in the bin.

Late into the night,
Jan sat in the dark
and held her breath.
She listened to every sound,
and every sound was another break-in.

All she could think was:
what if they come back?

# CHAPTER THREE

The next night,
at about half-past six,
a man came and knocked on Jan's front door.

He was small and thin, all skin and bone,
in shabby jacket and jeans.

He had put on a cheap, thin tie
for this special occasion.

He stood looking up at Jan,
in the warm light of her home.
For a second,
she thought he was afraid of her.

"I'm from Victim Support," he said.
"The police told us you were burgled..."

Jan frowned, and said nothing.

"I've come to see if I can help.
In any way."
Still Jan said nothing.

"Would you like to talk?" he went on,
"It might help, you know...
Are you having trouble sleeping?"

"Yes," she said at last.
"I can't sleep at all.
Why are you here?" she asked him.

"I want to make sure you're all right,"
he said, and it was the truth.

"Can I come in?
We could talk...
I'm sorry about what happened..."

"I'm sorry too..." she said at last.
"Yes. Why not. Come on in."

She held the door wide
and watched him walk in.

He went straight into the living room,
where Dazz had gone to work
the night before.
Shelves stood empty
where Jan's things had been.

"What did they take?" he asked.

"Stereo," said Jan. "Video. A few CDs.
The usual. You should know."

"Yes, I suppose so," said the man.
"But you can replace all those things, can't you?
With insurance...

"I just hope you never lost nothing sentimental,"
he went on, "nothing personal..."

"I lost a lot of sleep," Jan snapped,
"that's personal. I lost confidence,
I'm scared to go out and leave the house,
and I don't want to live here any more.
I lost a lot of things."

"I just thought," he mumbled,
"Well... maybe you'd be grateful...
they were quite kind to you, in a way..."

"I hate the people who did this!"
She was angry now.

"Don't you understand?
They've been in my house!
They've taken my things!"

"Well maybe they've got nothing!"
he shouted back, "No money, no job!
Maybe they've got bills to pay!
Maybe they don't like the work,
but it's the only work they can get!"

He stopped, and looked at her,
afraid again.

"I must go," he said,
"I won't keep you..."

At the door, he turned and said:
"There's just one thing.
Could you let me have
a photograph of you...
For our files...
We keep files, at the office.
If you've got a photo, that is..."

"Mm. Yes." she said.
"I think I can find you one.
Can you come back tomorrow night?
About the same time?
You can pick it up then."

"Okay," he said, "I will!"
and he smiled like a little boy.

Then – "Thank you" – he added,
and disappeared, like a thief,
like a shadow,
into the night.

# CHAPTER FOUR

All that night,
and all the next day,
I was kicking myself:

Fool! Fool! Stupid, stupid fool!
Can't you do anything right?

In my dreams,
I say the right things,
in all the right places,
but in real life, it comes out wrong.

Why didn't I ask her out?
When she was being so nice,
when she said "come back tomorrow night",
I could have said: "why not go for a drink?"

And she would say: "Yes, I'd like that!"

And why didn't I find out about this David?
Is he still her boyfriend, or what?

And she would say:
"No, it's all over between us.
Right now, I'm looking for somebody new..."

And then she would look at me,
just like in that photograph.

But all my plans went wrong last night.
I talked too much,
I said stupid things.

I wanted Jan to understand me.
I wanted her to know what it's like
to have nothing,
when everyone else around you
has got everything.
Jobs and money.

I wanted her to know me
but I almost gave it all away.

But as I walked to her house, the next night,
I was thinking: tonight will be different.

Tonight – no mistakes.
This time, I will keep cool.

She will open the door
and smile with her beautiful eyes,
and say:
"I'm so glad you came back!"

She will give me that photograph of her,
the first time I saw her,
and I will say: "Thank you, Jan.
Now let me take you for a drink..."

But all my plans went wrong.
Again.
As usual.

When I got there, and knocked,
it took her ages to come to the door.

"Oh it's you," she said,
"I'm glad you came back. Come on in."

She was trying to sound nice,
but her eyes were cold and hard.

For a second, I almost turned and ran.
I don't know why.
Something made me want to run away.

But I stood looking up at Jan,
and I wanted her so much.
The feeling was so strong,
I knew I would never run away again.

I stepped into the house.
"You look tired," I said softly.
"Let me..." I went to stroke her face,
but she pushed my hand away.

"No! Go in..." she said.

Jan shut the front door,
and I went into the living room.
There were two policemen in there.
I heard Jan slide the bolt on the door.

"Sit down, son."

I heard a policewoman with Jan in the hall.
She was on the radio,
telling the cars to come and pick us up.

I sat down.

They stood over me.
"I don't suppose
you have anything you'd like to tell us,
have you, kid...?"

"I didn't take nothing..." I began,
"I just wanted to see her again.
You see,
we were growing fond of each other..."

On the way out,
we passed Jan in the hall.

The look she gave me:
so much hate.

For the first time in years,
I felt like crying.

The policeman was saying:
"Your first mistake, last night,
was saying you were from Victim Support.
The woman from Victim Support got there
half an hour before you...

"Your second mistake," he went on.
"When Jan let you in,
you went straight into the living room.
You knew your way around,
because you had been before..."

"But your big mistake," said Jan,
"was wanting me to like you,
to feel sorry for you,
to understand and pity you.

"You broke in and took my things,
then you came back
because you wanted me, too..."

"But I'm in love with you!" I cried.

But the police were pushing me out to the cars,
and Jan was shutting her door,
and she was talking to the policewoman again,
and she didn't seem to see me, or hear me...

...and the night was full of crackling radios
and the blue lights swept across the houses
and across the white faces of the policemen...

...and strong hands bent me,
and pushed me into a car, and held me,
and I didn't have time to turn and look back
before they slammed all the doors
and drove me away.